ST ISAAC'S CATHEDRAL

LENINGRAD

ST ISAAC'S CATHEDRAL

LENINGRAD

Aurora Art Publishers · Leningrad

COMPILED AND INTRODUCED
BY GEORGY BUTIKOV

TRANSLATED FROM THE RUSSIAN
BY DAVID AND JUDITH ANDREWS

DESIGNED BY VALENTIN VESELKOV
AND NIKOLAI KUTOVOI

St Isaac's, one of the finest cathedrals built in Europe in the nineteenth century, is a unique phenomenon in Russian architecture. A characteristic feature of its decoration is the use of different forms of monumental art—sculpture, painting, and mosaics—which combine to form an overall unity of great artistic power. The tall, centrally planned, domed Cathedral is one of the buildings which punctuate the skyline of Leningrad.

The Cathedral is a dominant feature of two great ensembles, St Isaac's Square and Decembrists' (formerly Senate) Square, and to a large extent determines their general character by its monumental architectural form.

The existing Cathedral is the fourth church to be constructed in this area. All of them were dedicated to St Isaac the Dalmatian, the legendary Byzantine monk, also known as St Isaac of Constantinople and called "Dalmatian" from the name later given to the monastery which he had founded. The construction of each of the four churches was closely related to the history of the city and reflected the different architectural, artistic, and town-planning trends of the periods in which they were built.

When Peter the Great founded St Petersburg in 1703, he made a decision to erect in his new city a cathedral to St Isaac the Dalmatian, whose feast-day, May 30, coincided with Peter's birthday. Seven years later, in 1710, a small wooden church was built on the Admiralty Green near the site of the present-day Cathedral. On February 19, 1712, Peter the Great and Catherine had their public wedding there (they had been married privately several years before). This building, unassuming as it was in design and decoration, was felt to be out of keeping with the grand scale on which the new capital of Russia was being constructed. On August 6, 1717, on the bank of the Neva where the Bronze Horseman, a monument to Peter the Great, now stands, the foundations were laid for a second church of St Isaac, which was designed by Johann Mattarnovi. Its architecture was reminiscent of the SS Peter and Paul Cathedral in St Petersburg, the work of Domenico Trezzini. The identical principle of design, similar bell-towers with clocks on them, and carved gilt iconostases inside, both designed by Ivan Zarudny, made the affinity between the two structures even more striking. The site selected for the church proved unsuitable; the ground on the unfortified Neva banks began to shift and cracks developed in the building's walls and vaults. The work of destruction was completed by a fire in 1735. In an attempt to restore the cathedral, the architects built the dome without a spire and on a much smaller scale, so as to reduce the pressure on the walls and vaults; the bell-tower was not rebuilt at all, and as a result the edifice gave the impression of being unfinished. In 1763 it was demolished.

On July 15, 1761, the building of a new St Isaac's was entrusted by a special decree of the Senate to the architect Savva Chevakinsky, who was then completing the construction of the Cathedral of St Nicholas of Myra, a remarkable example of Russian eighteenth-century architecture. Chevakinsky chose for the building a site much farther up the bank — the same, in fact, where the Cathedral now stands. Catherine II, who came to the throne in 1762, approved the idea of re-creating the cathedral which was associated with the name of Peter the Great, and agreed with the site chosen by Chevakinsky, but she entrusted the task of planning and building the new church to another architect, Antonio Rinaldi. According to his design, the new cathedral was to have five cupolas of elaborate shape, and a tall stately bell-tower; a marble facing was to lend subtlety of colour to its four façades. The building could have become one of the finest creations by the noted "master of marble façades" but the work moved very slowly and Rinaldi, who was obliged to leave St Petersburg, did not see it completed. A model executed after Rinaldi's design (now in the Museum of the Academy of Arts, Leningrad) gives an idea of the beauty of the cathedral as it would have been, had Rinaldi's project been realized.

After Catherine's death Paul I, dissatisfied with the slow rate of progress, instructed the architect Vincenzo Brenna, put in charge of the project, to complete the work with all possible speed. In order to do this Brenna was forced to distort Rinaldi's design by reducing the proportions of the upper part of the cathedral and by building one cupola instead of five. The marble facing extended only to the cornices, which left the brickwork of the upper portion of the building exposed. The church finished in 1802 was squat and clumsy, and the contemporaries found it ridiculous. The following anecdote is illustrative of the manners of the period. A young naval officer on first seeing St Isaac's composed an epigram in this vein:

> Two emperors' relique,
> It is by nature double:
> Its foundation is of marble
> And crown, of brick.

The first (wooden) St Isaac's Church. 1710. Lithograph

Late at night, when trying to affix the paper with the verse onto the façade of the cathedral, he was observed and arrested. The officer paid dearly for his display of wit: he had his tongue and ears cut off and was then sent to Siberia. The cathedral was felt to be so much out of harmony with the splendour of the capital that seven years later, in 1809, the question of rebuilding it arose again. A competition was held for the best design. Count Alexander Stroganov, then President of the Academy of Arts, drew up a programme for the competition which stipulated, on the order of Alexander I, that the eastern part of Rinaldi's church should be incorporated in the new building.

Among those who submitted their designs for the competition in 1809 and 1813 were Adrian Zakharov, Andrei Voronikhin, Vasily Stasov, Giacomo Quarenghi, and other prominent architects. Most of them, however, suggested demolishing the old cathedral, which was contrary to the wishes of Alexander I.

The events of 1812, when Napoleon crossed the Russian frontier and the Patriotic War began, put an end to all debate. It was only two or three years after the victory that discussions were resumed, which resulted in the decision to rebuild the cathedral. The design and building of the fourth St Isaac's Cathedral were entrusted to Auguste Ricard de Montferrand, a young architect who had completed a course of studies at the Ecole Royale et spéciale d'architecture in Paris with distinction and had had some practical training at the studio of the famous French architects, Charles Percier and Pierre Fontaine. In 1816 Montferrand came to Russia where he was to spend the greater part of his life, becoming with time one of the most prominent architects of his age. Because of his undisputed talent, combined with a breadth of artistic vision and an unlimited ability to perfect his mastery of architecture and building techniques, Montferrand was able to direct this vast project for more than forty years, despite occasional mistakes and failures. His success was considerably facilitated by the work of a Committee set up by the Academy of Arts, which included Carlo Rossi, Vasily Stasov, Abram Melnikov, Andrei Mikhailov, Alexander Mikhailov, and other prominent Russian architects. The members of the Committee took an active part in the solution of all principal architectural and engineering problems. As a matter of fact, Montferrand's way of work largely depended on his ability to estimate the practical value and to make use of the suggestions and experience of those who worked with him.

St Isaac's owes its beauty and grandeur to the work of many architects, engineers, sculptors, and painters who built and decorated it; but it also absorbed the efforts of thousands of serfs and corvée workers who toiled thirteen to sixteen hours a day without holidays. The number of people who died from ill health, epidemic diseases and accidents is estimated, on the basis of the surviving records, at about one hundred thousands. The fire gilding of the main and the minor domes alone cost dozens of lives: the workmen died in torments from

8

The third St Isaac's Church. Designed by Antonio Rinaldi. 1768.
Drawing by Auguste Montferrand

mercury vapour poisoning. It is justly said that St Isaac's stands on the bones of its serf builders.

The construction of the grandiose cathedral was an important event in the life of the capital. The inhabitants of St Petersburg, common folk and members of the upper classes alike, followed each stage of the work with avid attention. One of the episodes which aroused general interest was the arrival from the Pytärlaks quarry, and the unloading at the Neva embankment, of forty-eight huge monolithic granite columns for the porticoes. A contemporary, the French traveller Dupré de Saint-Maure, who was then in St Petersburg, describes his impressions thus: "A fine spectacle, the unloading of the first six columns...

9

The third St Isaac's Church. Completed to a design by Vincenzo Brenna. 1802

intended for the porticoes of the new temple... During several days a mood of expectation reigned in the city. An enormous crowd gathered on the embankment and in St Isaac's Square to witness the marvel... This feat is a triumph of human endurance, strength, and knowledge." Another account was left us by Nikolai Bestuzhev, a gifted journalist and painter, a republican who was later to take part in the insurrection of December 14, 1825. In one of his essays he rebukes the editors of Russian newspapers and magazines for failing to accord proper praise to this truly popular feat: "We search for wonders in strange lands; we avidly peruse ancient histories recording the titanic deeds of Architecture in olden times, and exclaim at every line: marvellous! unbelievable!.. And we pass by these marvellous, unbelievable columns with no more than common curiosity... The huge size of these columns, the simple methods which Nature herself has taught to our common folk... all this fills my heart with a pleasant feeling..."

The four decades which it took to build St Isaac's, 1818 to 1858, formed an epoch in the development of Russian architecture and building techniques. Structural problems, which arose in the course of the work, were solved with the participation of such leading engineers and mathematicians of the age as Augustin Béthencourt, Karl Oppermann, Léon Carbonier, Piotr Lomnovsky, Gabriel Lamé, and Pierre Clapeyron.

The beginning of the works coincided with the flowering of Classicism in Russia. The middle of the nineteenth century saw, however, the first symptoms of a gradual decline in Late Classical architecture, marked by a breakdown of stylistic purity, a departure from the principle of architectural and decorative unity. A tendency developed to overload the buildings with purely ornamental detail which had no structural meaning. These features heralded the beginning of Eclecticism in architecture. St Isaac's, the last major building in Russia designed in the style of Late Classicism, already shows an influence of this new trend. The building was conceived as a compact volume with the façades decorated by huge Corinthian porticoes that lend the Cathedral an austere dignity. The smooth surfaces of the walls faced with grey marble are broken up by large arched windows with massive surrounds, and the corners of the main block are decorated with pilasters. The Cathedral is surmounted by a tall drum crowned by a gilt dome with an octagonal lantern; four turrets by the sides of the drum serve as bell-towers.

The clarity of the basic volumes is somewhat marred by the heavy magnificence of the window surrounds and the excessive use of sculpture on the pediments. This does not, however, prevent St Isaac's, with its striking monumental power, from being one of the most interesting structures in the city. Its noble grandeur has frequently been noted, researchers particularly commenting on the strong impression produced by the huge granite columns, and the subtlety of plastic and colour effects resulting from the combination of the different architectural elements: the pediments, statues, bell-towers, and dome.

The statues and reliefs which adorn the building form one of the largest groups of sculpture created in the nineteenth century. The works decorating the balustrade of the drum, the pediments and outer doors were done by the outstanding sculptors Ivan Vitali and Peter Klodt, and also by Joseph Hermann, Philippe Lemaire, and Alexander Loganovsky.

11

Quarrying granite and shaping the columns for St Isaac's at Pytärlaks.
Drawing by Auguste Montferrand

The distribution of the sculptures corresponds to the basic sections of the building. Here they unite the architectural masses by softening the transition from one section to another, there they heighten the expressiveness of the individual elements of architecture. Hermann's statues of angels on the balustrade, while emphasizing the elegant form of the drum and the rhythm of the dome's articulation, serve to link the drum to the dome; and the groups of angels with torches, the work of Vitali, link the basic volume of the church to its crowning parts, the drum and the dome.

The four large high reliefs in the tympana of the pediments are of particular interest. The relief of the south portico, created by Vitali, depicts the *Adoration of the Magi*. The triangular contours of the pediment set the pattern of the composition, which is arranged strictly according to the laws of symmetry,

12

Unloading the columns at the Neva embankment.
Lithograph from a drawing by Auguste Montferrand

with the main protagonist, Mary, an ideal of perfect female beauty, occupying the central position. The figures of the Magi, sculpted nearly in the round, are more realistic in treatment. We know that Vitali made the heads of the Ethiopian King and his page from life: Abyssinian servants on the staff of the imperial household posed for him.

In the high relief of the west pediment with the scene of *St Isaac Blessing the Emperor Theodosius*, Vitali added to the main characters, who are treated conventionally, several figures representing his own contemporaries. For example, in the members of the Emperor's entourage, Victor and Saturninus, one can recognize Prince Peter Volkonsky, Chairman of the Commission for the Construction of St Isaac's, and Alexei Olenin, President of the Academy of Arts. Montferrand, clad in a toga, reclines in a corner of the pediment, holding a

13

model of St Isaac's in his hand. His face is somewhat idealized and his pose full of dignity. His powerful figure, however, appears too large for the corner of the tympanum.

The north pediment is decorated with a high relief of the *Resurrection* by Lemaire, while the east pediment bears his *St Isaac Accosts the Emperor Valens*.

Figures of the Apostles and Evangelists, which mark the apices and corners of the pediments, serve to complete the composition. This function dictated the character of their treatment: their sharp and clear contours, their monumental forms, and the flowing lines of their clothes suggesting movement.

The Cathedral's interior, which is decorated with paintings, mosaics, and sculptures, impresses the viewer by its majestic architecture, and by the variety of colour effects produced by a combination of marble, semiprecious stones, and gilding. 400 kilograms of gold and 1,000 tons of ormolu went into the decoration of the Cathedral. 16,000 kilograms of malachite and over eleven square metres of lapis lazuli from Badakhshan were used for the facing of the columns and other architectural details of the chancel and the two chapels. The floors, walls, and piers are lined with semiprecious Shoksha porphyry, with black slate from the Caucasus, and different marbles: pink Tivdiya marble, grey marble from Finland, white Italian marble, green marble from Genoa, yellow marble from Siena, and red marble from France. Academician Alexander Fersman, the eminent mineralogist of our time, described St Isaac's as a treasury of Russian coloured stones, second only to the Hermitage in the wealth and variety of materials. The final version of his design for the Cathedral's interior was completed by Montferrand in 1842. While the arrangement of sculptures in the main dome follows a Classical pattern, the decoration of the vaults is in the Baroque style, and the inner doors show a marked influence of the Italian Renaissance.

The chancel and chapels, parts of the interior intended to produce the strongest effect, are decorated with particular splendour. Precious materials are lavishly used to achieve rich harmonies of colour, and a striking unity of impression is attained in the combined employment of painting, mosaics, and sculpture. The iconostasis of the chancel, faced with white marble, is adorned with ten pillars of malachite and two of lapis lazuli; the latter are among the foremost of the rarities to be seen in the Cathedral. The icons of the first and second tiers are mosaic, while those of the third tier are painted. The icons of the

14

Auguste Ricard de Montferrand (1786—1858). Lithograph

first tier, executed after the paintings by Timoleon Karl von Neff, depict the patron saints of the Tsars during whose reigns the Cathedral was built. The mosaics of the second tier, executed after the pictures by Fiodor Briullov, one of the outstanding Russian painters of the academic school, are dedicated to the patron saints of the members of the imperial family. The painted icons of the third tier, which are the work of Semion Zhivago, represent Old Testament prophets. Above the chancel arch is the ormolu group of *Christ in Glory* done by Peter Klodt.

Beyond the Holy Gate, in the half-dark of the sanctuary, is a stained-glass window which depicts the risen Christ. This window was made in 1841—43 to the design of Leo von Klenze at the Royal Works in Munich, where the finest masters of stained glass worked at the time. The head of the Works was Max Emmanuel Einmiller and it seems likely that he took a personal part in fulfilling such an important commission.

The side arches that break up the main iconostasis lead to the chapels. They are splendidly decorated with a variety of fine materials. The iconostases of white Italian marble have panels of malachite and other coloured stones and are in no way inferior to the main iconostasis as regards artistic perfection. The greyish pink marble facing in the east part of the chapels, preserved from the third cathedral designed by Rinaldi, is remarkable for the noble beauty of its muted colours. It sets off to great advantage the white marble facing of the iconostases and the walls which separate the chapels from the main sanctuary. The gilt sculptured groups of *The Resurrection* and *The Transfiguration*, by Nikolai Pimenov, complete the decoration of the chapels. The décor of the chancel and chapels is of undoubted interest, despite an obvious lack of stylistic unity. The drum of the dome is a splendid example of a synthesis of sculpture and architecture: the twelve statues of angels, which continue the rhythm of the verticals created by the pilasters, emphasize the lofty proportions of the Cathedral. Most of the statues which decorate the vaults are the work of Vitali. The figures of prophets, patriarchs, and angels are strongly foreshortened, their proportions deliberately distorted to be better perceived from below. The shallow niches of the vaults seem cramped, and this creates a tension which strengthens the dynamic quality of the composition.

The reliefs of Vitali on the three great inner doors are reminiscent in their composition of the "Golden Doors" of the Florence Baptistery, designed and executed by Lorenzo Ghiberti. The reliefs of the great north door illustrate the legends of St Isaac the Dalmatian and St Nicholas of Myra in Lycia, while those of the south door show events from the history of Ancient Russia, and the west doors are dedicated to the lives of SS Peter and Paul. The scenes in the panels are arranged in three planes, the setting barely indicated, the middle ground in low and the foreground in high relief. This is done with great skill, so as to achieve a sense of deep space without destroying the plane of the door. Many of the characters of these expressive sculptural compositions are treated in a realistic style: the busts of St Nonna and St Theodore the Martyr on the

St Isaac's Cathedral. 1818—58. Designed by Auguste Montferrand. 1825.
Lithograph from a drawing by Auguste Montferrand

north door and those of Princess Fevronia and St Michael of Chernigov on
the south door are testimony to the sculptor's effort to depart from the academic canon, and his attempts to represent men and women realistically.

The magnificent gilt capitals and bases of the columns and pilasters, the glit-
tering balustrade, the openwork railing with its elaborate fanciful design of
meander and plant motifs, a wealth of ornamental detail on the vaults, the intri-
cate pattern of the gilt Holy Gate — all this can hardly be said to form a unity:
the interior is certainly overcrowded with ornamentation. Yet, on close inspection each individual detail strikes us by its perfect design and expert execution.
The Cathedral contains more than one hundred and fifty murals and pictures
in oils, a unique collection of Russian monumental painting of the first half
of the nineteenth century. They were done by well-known Russian artists of
the academic school — Karl Briullov, Fiodor Bruni, Nikolai Alexeyev, Vasily

17

Shebuyev, Piotr Basin, and others. Montferrand was responsible for the overall arrangement of the murals, while Vasily Shebuyev, a prominent Russian artist, Professor and President of the Academy of Arts, superintended work on the paintings. The pictures in the west part of the Cathedral are devoted to Old Testament subjects, while those in its east portion deal with New Testament themes. The ceiling of the main dome was painted by Briullov, though he did not live to complete it. A grave illness forced him to leave for Italy where he died soon afterwards. Basin completed the work, following Briullov's cartoons and studies. The ceiling is one of the most outstanding large-scale decorative works in the Classical style.

The test of the artist's mastery in monumental painting is his ability to capture the main features of the subject, avoiding excessive detail and using broad, free brush-strokes. Briullov was a consummate master of this technique. The Virgin on her throne is surrounded by saints and angels who are painted in various complicated foreshortened positions. The outlines of the figures are austere and at the same time highly expressive; the colouring is wonderfully joyful and radiant. Briullov used to say: "I want everything I do to be suffused with light." And it is true that, looking at the painting even on overcast days, you feel the depth of celestial space, full of light and air, and the weightlessness of the figures soaring in it. The soft yet bright colours give it a highly decorative quality and superbly unite the ceiling with the sumptuous architecture and sculpture of the interior. In the drum of the dome, between the figures of angels, are the Twelve Apostles, painted by Basin after Briullov's cartoons. The paintings on the vaults are the work of the eminent Russian artist Fiodor Bruni. One of his most interesting works in St Isaac's is the painting in the central section, representing the *Vision of the Prophet Ezekiel*. The overall blue-grey tone serves to unite the figures: the sombre colours emphasize the underlying idea of the painting which is a hymn to the might of God. The same theme of God's omnipotence is dominant in Bruni's murals of *The Last Judgement* and *The Flood*. However, in *The Flood* — Bruni's best work in the Cathedral — the subject has a different emphasis: here it is mankind, suffering in a horrible calamity sent by the will of God, that is the centre of interest and the object of the author's sympathies. The scene depicts a group of people at a cliff-top, surrounded by the raging elements, and trying to escape the dreadful fate that awaits them. The artist painted only nine figures, but the tragic depths of the catastrophe which befell the whole mankind are nevertheless conveyed with great power and expressiveness. The artistic language of the painting is sparing and concise, the details carefully chosen, and the figures treated in a generalized manner. The balanced rhythm of the composition and Bruni's characteristic blue-grey colour range serve to create a mood of tragic hopelessness. Outstanding among the paintings decorating the attic is Alexeyev's picture *The Crossing of the Red Sea*, a dramatic composition with intense colouring and a wealth of detail. The figure of the Prophet Moses, dignified and solemn, dominates the scene; its importance is emphasized by the use of tense, vivid colours. Of interest among the murals of the attic are the works of Basin, Shebuyev, Alexei Markov, Fiodor Zavyalov, and Piotr Shamshin.

The pictures placed in the niches of the piers are by Timoleon Karl von Neff, Charles de Steuben, and Cesare Mussini. The richly ornamented frames of white Carrara marble give a monumental quality to these works, originally executed as easel paintings. The most interesting of them are Neff's *Presentation of the Virgin* and Steuben's *Crucifixion*.

The figures of Joachim, Anna, and the High Priest Zaccharias in the *Presentation of the Virgin* are painted rather traditionally and lack emotion; but a skilful use of chiaroscuro in the architectural background creates a sense of the depth of space and enhances the solemn mood pervading the picture, giving at the same time a warm lyrical charm to the gentle figure of the Virgin.

Steuben's *Crucifixion*, executed according to the precepts of the academic school, is enlivened by a certain Romantic quality, particularly prominent in the strong contrasts of light and shade that stem from Caravaggio. The problem of colour is successfully solved: a unity of colouring is achieved by the use of a soft shade of brown which links the bright patches of local colour in the clothing, and of soft background tones which harmonize with it.

Alongside with paintings, mosaic pictures were widely used in interior decoration. The necessity to resort to this technique, which Vasari had aptly described as "eternal painting", arose in connection with quick deterioration of oil paintings caused by an imperfect system of ventilation and heating. It was Montferrand who suggested that some of the pictures should be replaced by their copies in mosaics. The work, started in 1851, was finished in 1917. The artists

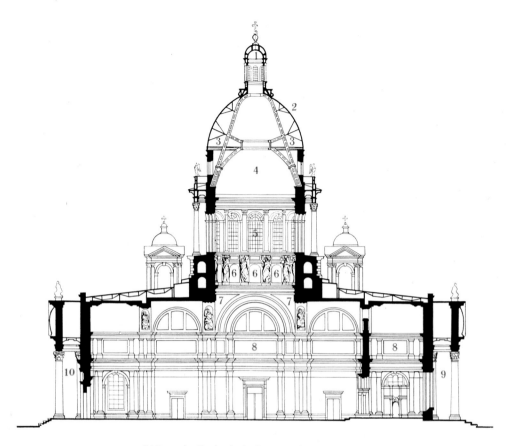

St Isaac's Cathedral. Longitudinal section

1. Lantern; 2. Dome; 3. Framework of the dome; 4. Ceiling of the dome;
5. Drum of the dome; 5 *The Twelve Apostles*: painted decoration; 7. Vaults;
8 Attic; 9. East portico; 10. West portico

Vasily Rayev, Yegor Solntsev, Ivan Shapovalov, and Stepan Fiodorov, gradu-
ates of the Academy, then on their Roman tour, were directed, on Montferrand's
suggestion, to stay there for an additional term to train in the art of mosaic
work under the famous mosaicist Michelangelo Barberi. In the middle of the
nineteenth century the Roman mosaic was generally accepted as a technique
best suited to making copies of oil paintings and enabling the artist to create
a mosaic version closely reproducing the original picture.

Among the paintings replaced by mosaics were those in the first and second
tiers of the iconostases, and the murals in the central section of the building:
The Passion and the *Four Evangelists* in the pendentives. The first mosaic to
be executed was *The Saviour* in the main iconostasis (after the painting by Neff).
One of the best mosaics is *St Catherine* in the south-east chapel, after the paint-

20

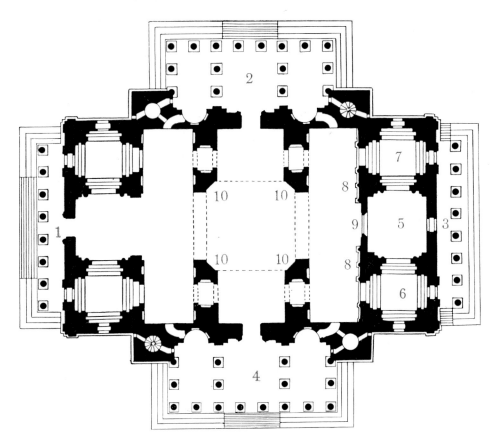

St Isaac's Cathedral. Plan

1. West portico; 2. North portico; 3. East portico; 4. South portico;
5. Chancel; 6. St Catherine's Chapel; 7. St Alexander Nevsky's Chapel;
8. The main iconostasis; 9. The Holy Gate; 10. Piers carrying the main dome

ed original by Neff. The inlay work is done with such meticulous accuracy that the icon, even when viewed at close quarters, seems to have been painted. The play of light and shade and the texture of different objects — the cold glint of metal, the sheen of the satin robes, and the living warmth of a human hand — are all captured perfectly. In their efforts to reproduce exactly the wealth of colour which distinguished the painted original, the artists made use of smalts of more than twelve thousand different shades.

The Last Supper, a mosaic in the chancel made after the painting by Zhivago, is interesting for the skilful application of a technique of the optical mixture of colours: pieces of variously coloured smalt were chosen in such a way that at a distance their colours blend into the required tone. Judas' white cloak is an excellent example of this: on closer inspection we see that the smalts used here are of a great variety of tones — greenish, yellowish, bluish, and others. The mosaics of the late nineteenth and early twentieth centuries were made in a technique different from the one used in the iconostases. It is exemplified by the mosaic copy of *St Peter* which was intended for the drum of the dome and was thus designed to be viewed from a great distance. Its surface is left unpolished; the pieces of smalt, set at different angles and depths, form a vivid, uneven surface, with light playing on the edges of the tesserae.

Characteristically, most of the best mosaics in the Cathedral were made jointly by several masters. The expert supervision of Bruni and Alexander Frolov greatly contributed to their excellence.

At the London Exhibition of 1862 the mosaics of St Isaac's were highly praised. Specialists remarked that the production of smalts at the Russian mosaic works "had reached a degree of perfection attained nowhere else in Europe". The practice of mosaic work in St Isaac's played an important part in the revival of this art in Russia.

On May 30, 1858, the consecration ceremony was held, and St Isaac's became the principal cathedral church of the capital.

For some time after the October Revolution the Cathedral continued to operate. In 1931 St Isaac's was transformed into a museum by a decree of the Soviet Government. On its inauguration day the Soviet scientist, the astronomer Nikolai Kamenshchikov, staged here the world's largest experiment with the Foucault pendulum which demonstrates the earth's rotation on its axis, thereby providing visual proof of the theory of Nicolaus Copernicus.

During the War of 1941—45 the Museum did not work. The premises were used for storing art treasures and archives brought here from several palace museums in the environs of Leningrad. Sculptures, furniture, porcelains, and countless files of museum documents of great value were carefully preserved throughout the long and hard months of the Nazi blockade of Leningrad.

The Cathedral suffered heavy damage during the war years, particularly as regards its decoration. Restoration works conducted by a large body of Soviet architects, painters, mosaicists, and sculptors in the post-war period returned its former splendour to St Isaac's, this majestic edifice summing up the achievements in building techniques, architecture, and the various branches of the decorative art in Russia during the first half of the nineteenth century.

PLATES

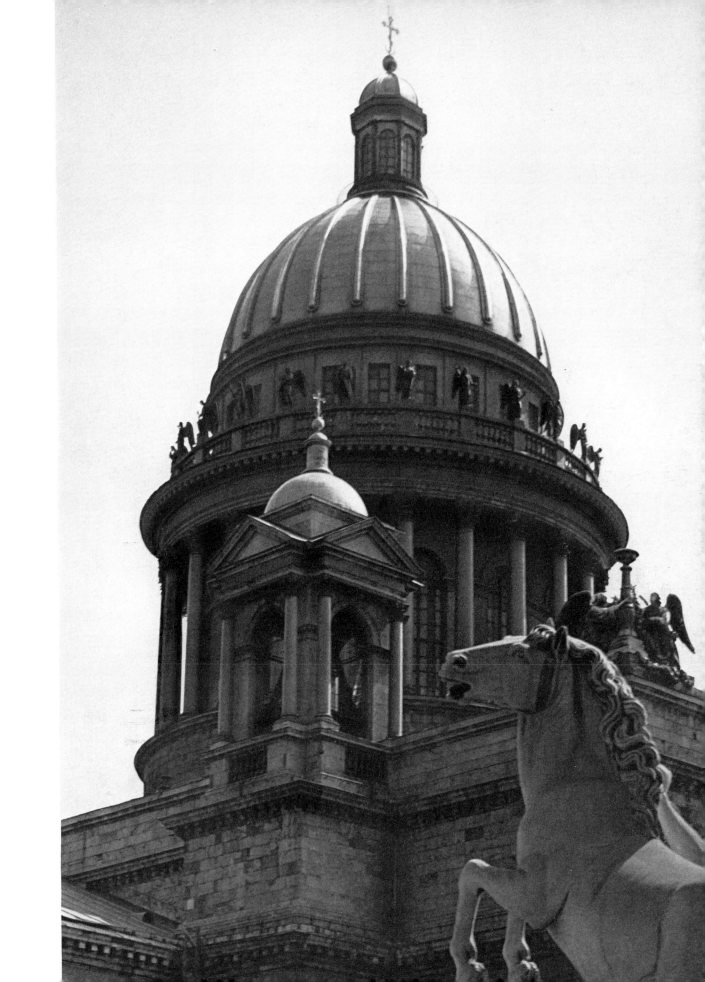

7
St Isaac's Square

8
St Isaac's Cathedral.
South façade

9
Portico of
the south façade

10
Drum of the main dome,
the bell-towers,
and the pediment
of the south portico

11--15 *Adoration of the Magi.* Relief
on the pediment of the south portico

16
St Philip. Statue
on the roof
of the south portico

17
*St Matthew
the Evangelist
and the Angel.*
Sculptural group
on the roof
of the south portico

18
Window surround

19
Slaughter of the Innocents. Relief in the south portico

20
St Isaac's Cathedral.
South and east façades

21
*St Isaac Accosts
the Emperor Valens.*
Relief on the pediment
of the east portico

22
St Luke the Evangelist.
Statue on the roof
of the east portico

23
South-east bell-tower

24
Colonnade of
the north portico

25 *The Resurrection.* Relief on the pediment of the north portico

26
Portico of
the west façade

27—30 *St Isaac Blessing the Emperor Theodosius and His Wife Flaccilla.*
Relief on the pediment of the west portico

31
*St Mark
the Evangelist.*
Statue on
the roof of
the west portico

32
*Angels
with a Torch.*
Sculptural group
over the attic

33
St Bartholomew.
Statue on the
roof of the west
portico

34
Colonnade
of the drum
of the main
dome

35
Balustrade
of the main
dome

36
South and west façades

43
Columns of
the main iconostasis

44
Christ. Stained glass
window in the
main sanctuary

45
The main iconostasis
of the Cathedral

46
St Catherine.
Icon of the main iconostasis

47
The Virgin and Child.
Icon of the main iconostasis

48, 49
St Nicholas.
Icon of the main iconostasis

50—52 *The Last Supper*.
Icon of the main iconostasis

53 The main iconostasis. Detail

54 The main iconostasis. Detail of decoration

55 The Holy Gate of the main sanctuary. Detail

56 *The Annunciation.* Mosaics on the Holy Gate
of the main sanctuary

57 The Holy Gate of the main sanctuary

58 Railing of the main sanctuary. Detail

59 Decoration of the main iconostasis. Detail

60 Base of a column of the main iconostasis

61 Iconostasis of St Catherine's Chapel

62 *The Resurrection*. Sculptural group over
the iconostasis of St Catherine's Chapel

63 *St Catherine*. Icon of the iconostasis
in St Catherine's Chapel

64 *St Anastasia*. Icon of the iconostasis
     in St Catherine's Chapel

65, 66 St Alexander Nevsky's Chapel.
         Marble décor

67
Iconostasis of
St Alexander
Nevsky's Chapel

68
The Transfiguration.
Sculptural group over
the iconostasis of
St Alexander
Nevsky's Chapel

69

Central part
of the Cathedral

70
The Last Judgement.
Painting on a vault in
the central part of the Cathedral

71—73
Vision of the Prophet Ezekiel.
Painting in the central part
of the Cathedral

74—76 *The Flood.* Painting in the attic of the west part of the nave

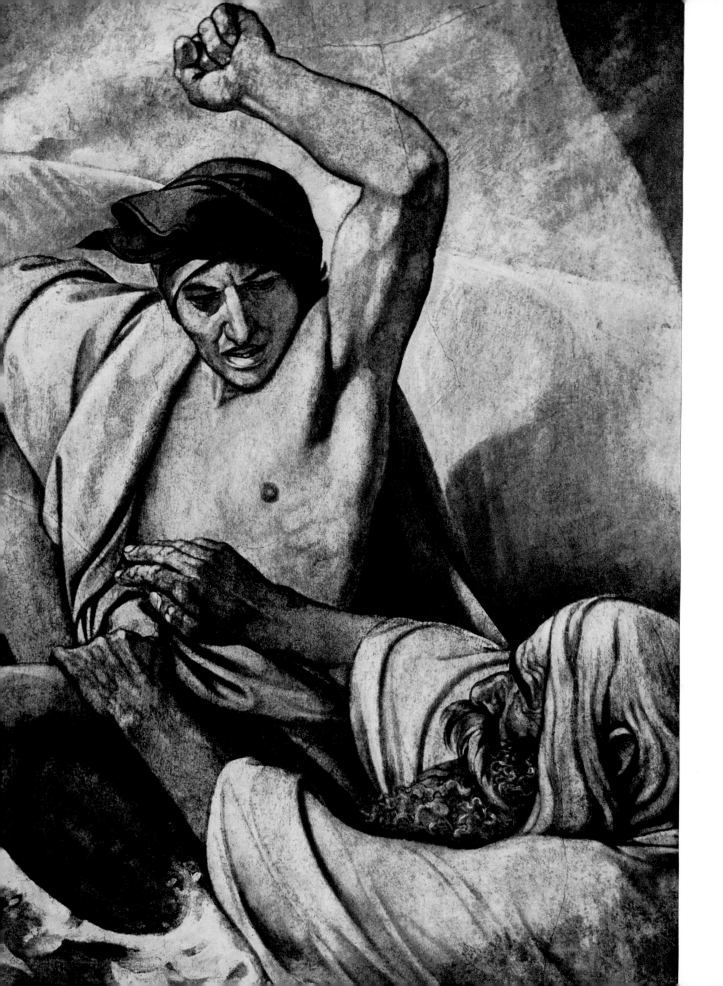

77—79 *The Crossing of the Red Sea.* Painting
in the north-west part of the Cathedral

80 *The Song of Miriam*. Painting in the attic
of the north-west part of the Cathedral

81 *The Betrayal.* Mosaics in the attic
of the central part of the Cathedral

82 *Christ Carrying the Cross.* Mosaics in the attic
of the central part of the Cathedral

83 *The Scourging of Christ.* Mosaics in the attic
of the central part of the Cathedral

84 *The Creation of the Sun and the Moon.* Painting
on a vault in the west part of the Cathedral

85
Decoration of
the vault of
the north aisle

86
*The Prophet
Ezekiel.*
Statue on a vault

87
*St Mark
the Evangelist.*
Mosaics in
the pendentive of
the main dome

88
*St John
the Evangelist.*
Mosaics in the
pendentive of
the main dome

89
Ceiling of
the main dome,
the drum,
and the pendentives

90, 91
Ceiling of the main dome

92–94
Drum of the main dome

95, 96
North aisle

97
Nativity of the Virgin.
Painting in the niche
of a pier

98
Presentation of the Virgin.
Painting in the niche
of a pier

99
South aisle

100
Chandelier

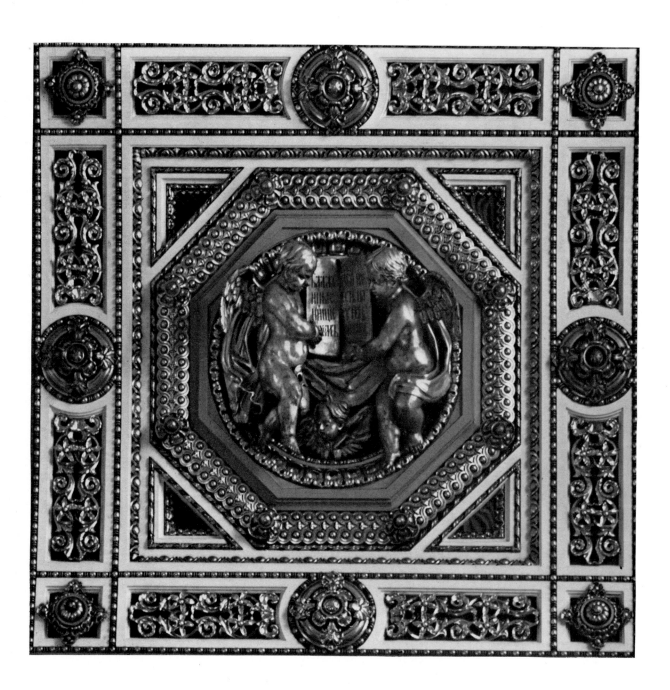

101, 102 Lesser vault of the south aisle.
Details of decoration

103—105 The great south inner door

NOTES ON THE PLATES

1—6 Views of St Isaac's Cathedral

7 St Isaac's Square

8 St Isaac's Cathedral. South façade. The Cathedral, 101.5 m high, is the fourth largest domed building in Europe (St Peter's in Rome is 143 m in height; St Paul's in London, 109 m; S. Maria del Fiore in Florence, 107 m). Weight, 300,000 tons. Area of more than one hectare

9 Portico of the south façade

10 Drum of the main dome, the bell-towers, and the pediment of the south portico

11 *Adoration of the Magi*. Relief on the pediment of the south portico. 1841—42. Bronze. Sculptor, Ivan Vitali. Central part

12 *The Virgin Mary*. Detail of the *Adoration of the Magi*

13 *St Joseph*. Detail of the *Adoration of the Magi*

14 *Presenting Gifts to the Christ Child*. Detail of the *Adoration of the Magi*

15 *The Ethiopian King's Page*. Detail of the *Adoration of the Magi*

16 *St Philip*. Statue on the roof of the south portico. 1842—44. Bronze. Height, 3.5 m. Sculptor, Ivan Vitali

17 *St Matthew the Evangelist and the Angel*. Sculptural group on the roof of the south portico. 1842—44. Bronze. Height, 3.5 m. Sculptor, Ivan Vitali

18 Window surround. Granite, marble. Area of window, 28.5 sq. m

19 *Slaughter of the Innocents*. Relief in the south portico. 1844—46. Bronze. Sculptor, Alexander Loganovsky

20 St Isaac's Cathedral. South and east façades

21 *St Isaac Accosts the Emperor Valens*. Relief on the pediment of the east portico. 1841—44. Sculptor, Philippe Lemaire

22 *St Luke the Evangelist*. Statue on the roof of the east portico. 1842—44. Bronze. Height, 3.5 m. Sculptor, Ivan Vitali

23 South-east bell-tower

24 Colonnade of the north portico. Granite. Weight of each column, 114 tons; height, 17 m; diameter, 1.8 m

25 *The Resurrection*. Relief on the pediment of the north portico. 1841—44. Sculptor, Philippe Lemaire

26 Portico of the west façade

27 *St Isaac Blessing the Emperor Theodosius and His Wife Flaccilla*. Relief on the pediment of the west portico. 1841—44. Bronze. Sculptor, Ivan Vitali

28 *Emperor Theodosius and Empress Flaccilla*. Detail of *St Isaac Blessing the Emperor Theodosius and His Wife Flaccilla*

29 *St Isaac*. Detail of *St Isaac Blessing the Emperor Theodosius and His Wife Flaccilla*

30 Figure of the architect Montferrand. Detail of *St Isaac Blessing the Emperor Theodosius and His Wife Flaccilla*

31 *St Mark the Evangelist*. Statue on the roof of the west portico. 1842—44. Bronze. Height, 3.5 m Sculptor, Ivan Vitali

162

71 *Vision of the Prophet Ezekiel*. Oil painting in the central part of the Cathedral. 1851—53. Area, 240 sq. m. Painter, Fiodor Bruni

72 *The Prophet Ezekiel*. Detail of the *Vision of the Prophet Ezekiel*

73 *Archangels*. Detail of the *Vision of the Prophet Ezekiel*

74 *The Flood*. Oil painting in the attic of the west part of the nave. 1843—47. Area, 23.27 sq. m. Painter, Fiodor Bruni

75 *The Flood*. Detail

76 *The Flood*. Detail

77 *The Crossing of the Red Sea*. Oil painting in the attic of the north-west part of the Cathedral. 1843—47. 10.7 × 3.7 m. Painter, Nikolai Alexeyev

78 *Moses*. Detail of *The Crossing of the Red Sea*

79 *Group of Israelites*. Detail of *The Crossing of the Red Sea*

80 *The Song of Miriam*. Oil painting in the attic of the north-west part of the Cathedral. 1844—50. 2.41 × 3.7 m. Painter, Fiodor Zavyalov

81 *The Betrayal*. Mosaics in the attic of the central part of the Cathedral. 1873—85. 3.7 × 2.65 m. After Piotr Basin's painted original

82 *Christ Carrying the Cross*. Mosaics in the attic of the central part of the Cathedral. 1873—85. 3.7 × 2.65 m. After Piotr Basin's painted original

83 *The Scourging of Christ*. Mosaics in the attic of the central part of the Cathedral. 1873—85. 3.7 × 2.65 m. After Piotr Basin's painted original

84 *The Creation of the Sun and the Moon*. Oil painting on a vault in the west part of the Cathedral. 1846—53. Area, 43.85 sq. m. Painter, Fiodor Bruni

85 Decoration of the vault of the north aisle. 1845—50. Sculptor, Ivan Vitali

86 *The Prophet Ezekiel*. Statue on a vault. 1845—50. Copper, gilt by the method of galvanoplasty. Sculptor, Ivan Vitali

87 *St Mark the Evangelist*. Mosaics in the pendentive of the main dome. 1887—96. Height, 5 m. After Piotr Basin's painted original

88 *St John the Evangelist*. Mosaics in the pendentive of the main dome. 1873—84. Height, 5 m. After Piotr Basin's painted original

89 Ceiling of the main dome, the drum, and the pendentives

90 Ceiling of the main dome. 1843—45. Oil painting. Area of more than 800 sq. m. Painter, Karl Briullov

91 Ceiling of the main dome. The central group: *The Virgin in Majesty*, detail of the painting

92 Drum of the main dome. Detail of decoration. Figures of angels executed in beaten copper and gilt by the method of galvanoplasty. Height of the figures, 5.5 m. Sculptor, Ivan Vitali. The Twelve Apostles between the figures of angels painted in oils by Basin after Briullov's cartoons

93 Drum of the main dome. Detail of decoration

94 Drum of the main dome. Detail of decoration: *Angel Holding the Tables of the Law*

95 North aisle. View from St Alexander Nevsky's Chapel

96 North aisle. View from the chancel

97 *Nativity of the Virgin*. Oil painting in the niche of a pier. 1846—48. 3.7 × 1.7 m. Painter, Timoleon Karl von Neff

98 *Presentation of the Virgin*. Oil painting in the niche of a pier. 1846—48. 3.7 × 1.7 m. Painter, Timoleon Karl von Neff

99 South aisle. View from St Catherine's Chapel

100 Chandelier. 1856—57. Gilt bronze. Weight, 2.5 tons. After a design by Auguste Montferrand

101 Lesser vault of the south aisle. Medallion in a caisson. Copper, gilt by the method of galvanoplasty

102 Lesser vault of the south aisle. Detail of decoration

103 The great south inner door. Oak, bronze. Area, 42 sq. m. Weight, 20 tons. Sculptor, Ivan Vitali

104 *St Alexander Nevsky Taking Monastic Vows before His Death*. Relief on the great south inner door. Bronze

105 *Peter the Great Bringing the Relics of St Alexander Nevsky to St Petersburg*. Relief on the great south inner door. Bronze

Photographs by Victor Khomenko (41, 43—53, 56, 58—64, 67, 68, 70—74, 76—83, 87—91, 96—99, 102, 105), Vladimir Shlakan (2, 3, 5, 7, 24, 26, 37, 39, 40, 54, 55, 57, 65, 66, 75, 84, 85, 92, 94, 95, 100, 101, 103), Mikhail Yeroshev (9, 16, 17, 22, 23, 25, 31, 33, 35, 38, 42, 69, 93, 104), Alexei Kazmin (12—15, 19, 28, 29, 32, 86), Victor Savik (10, 11, 18, 20, 27, 30, 36), Gleb Savin (8, 21, 34), Vladimir Samoilov (4), Vladimir Stukalov (1), and Boris Stukalov (6)

ИСААКИЕВСКИЙ СОБОР. ЛЕНИНГРАД
Альбом (на английском языке)
Издательство „Аврора". Ленинград. 1980
Изд. 2700. Printed and bound in the USSR